The Octagon of Spiritual Balances

PASTOR BERNARD J. WEATHERS

ISBN 978-1-68197-893-2 (Paperback)
ISBN 978-1-68197-895-6 (Hard Cover)
ISBN 978-1-68197-894-9 (Digital)

Christian Faith Publishing, Inc.
296 Chestnut Street
Meadville, PA 16335
www.christianfaithpublishing.com

All Bible verses were taken from the King James Version.

Printed in the United States of America

Contents

Rose Marie,

The love for God and His people is in your heart. May God continue to bless you.

Pastor Bernard

Bernard G. Weathers

Acknowledgements

I give all honor, praise and glory to God the Father, God the Son, and God the Holy Spirit; He who called me, died for me, and sealed me. I give thanks to my loving wife, Jo Anne for her prayers and standing in the gap for me, sanctifying me as a believing wife before I heard the voice of God. I like to thank my three daughters Shonda, Shereen, and Shavonne who know and understand me for the man I am today in God and not remembering me as the man I used to be.

Chapter 1

This chapter imparts a thorough explanation of the term spiritual balance. Faith, knowledge, and spiritual understanding are examined, and placed in their prospective positions as they originate in the life of the believer. It also produces a visual balance and profound understanding as it develops the desire and need, in the believer, to endure and progress in spiritual growth.

Chapter 2

Chapter 2 researches the balance of knowledge, faith, and belief which can only be attained when the preceding balance and factors are appropriated.

This chapter balances faith and belief as it defines belief in the spiritual sense; thereby, removing any preconceptions of man's control but promotes the power of the gospel, life in the word, and the manifestation of the work of the Holy Spirit.

Chapter 3

The third chapter encompasses the balancing of faith, belief, and trust. It defines belief and trust in a manner so closely associated that the word faith can be used inclusively.

The definition of trust is explained; its spiritual origin is reviewed, and its ill-effect on the other factors when not aligned appropriately within this balance is considered.

Chapter 4

This chapter introduces hope and confirms its existence. Hope is balanced with trust, defined, and applied both from a spiritual and carnal perspective.

Divine hope, which is an expected certainty, becomes discernible as the flagrant and deceptive work of Satan is revealed. The difference between godly and false hope is expounded.

Chapter 5

Chapter 5 orchestrates and introduces a balance of God's love in our lives, which creates a spiritually captivating appeal; therefore, promoting love and motivation in the life of the believer.

However, there are precautions and warnings of the devil's solicitations to deceive us in our true pursuit of experiencing God's love and operating in our love for Him.

Chapter 6

Our obedience is balanced with love in chapter 6; it explains why we must be certain that we are motivated by hearing directly from God and not of ourselves or the deception of Satan.

Obedience, as it applies in our spiritual walk, is shown to be the cornerstone of "The Octagon of Spiritual Balances," in as much as it fortifies and substantiates both, the preceding and subsequent balances.

Chapter 7

Chapter 7 is based upon obedience to the voice of God, and the search of true peace which surpasses human understanding. This chapter describes spiritual peace in contrast with the peace of this world.

It also reveals that the act of obedience, balanced with peace, will present purpose in the life of the believer.

Chapter 8

Chapter 8 introduces the balance of peace and joy. This final balance, when realized, experientially, is indicative of an achievement that will overwhelm the believer with such exultation, that the believer will emerge with a greater understanding and longing to continually seek and obey the word of God.

Introduction

The Octagon of Spiritual Balances was written and detailed for those who have been made aware of their salvation and are seeking the Christian way of life according to God's mandate as outlined in the Bible.

The focus is on the origin, sequence, and balancing of the spiritual attributes: faith, knowledge, spiritual understanding, belief, trust, hope, love, obedience, peace, and joy.

The purpose is to introduce and explain these spiritual attributes and their order of effective advent in the Christian life, instituting a spiritual foundation, awareness, and purpose in the believer, which, in due course, will create stability and harmony with God and life in the spirit.

It enhances the believer's understanding of the work and will of God in their lives and empowers them to discern and receive what is of and from God, opposed to deceptive enticements.

"The Octagon of Spiritual Balances" exposes the deceptive will of Satan and the manipulation of man's self-will.

When these ten factors/attributes are appropriated with the use of eight defined balances, a spiritual equilibrium is formed within the life of the believer.

This need is imperative for most of those within the body of Christ are sheeplike; they follow. Otherwise, they believe in and have a zeal for God but not according to spiritual understanding or knowledge. As a result they are more inclined to follow those who tend to intensify oratorical and theatrical abilities.

Upon reading this book, they will come to understand that the truth of God lies within our spirits. This is not a writing intended to criticize others; however, it is encouragement for the believer to look within his or her spirit where God the Holy Spirit resides and allow Him to present spiritual understanding, order, and purpose in their lives.

There are more Christians deceived today than any other time. The enemy is performing his job exceedingly well, in both our Bible studies and pulpits, through men and women who are viewed as being spiritual. Nonetheless, far too many of them fall short by beguiling enticements; therefore, they can only execute the same seducement.

"The Octagon of Spiritual Balances" cannot replace the word of God; however, it will help to place the word of God, in the believer's life, according to God's will. It causes the believer to seek for the truth within himself; therefore, receiving a greater and closer relationship with Jesus as well as a spiritual understanding, an understanding that can only come from the indwelling Holy Spirit.

The reader will come to understand that we, the believers, are vessels for the Holy Spirit to perform the expressed will of God both in and through us.

The believer will receive direction, purpose, spiritual clarity, and understanding as well as a confirmed spiritual equilibrium for Christian living. The reward and end result from following Jesus will be illuminated so vividly in the spirit of the believing reader that the reality of eternity will displace the thoughts of temporal time.

The word balance used in this book is not to be confused with the definition to bind as in a yoke or to weigh as with a pair of scales but rather to enhance and promote stability and harmony between two or more factors in the Christian's life therefore producing a spiritual equilibrium in the life of the Christian.

They are called spiritual balances because they originate from God and are produced in man to create stability and harmony in the Christian's walk.

These spiritual balances come from God, so they must be received in the spirit of man. Man cannot generate the gift of balance on his own!

God's spiritual balances will subsequently produce life, awareness, and an understanding in our spirits, and the application of this understanding empowers control over our soul and flesh; therefore, a balance is formed in the life of the Christian. Three factors construct a spiritual balance; awareness, spiritual understanding, and the application of the same. However, our spiritual balance starts with God, and accordingly, being spiritual, it cannot be constructed by man; rather, it must be generated in man.

God the Holy Spirit revealed these spiritual balances to me little by little throughout my Christian walk. I would like to confer with you how God prepared me to receive this blessing to share with you.

It started before the foundation of the world, but it was in 1990 when God called me. I was in the corporate realm of life, and I was making things happen for myself, so I believed.

Although I believed that there was a God, I really did not believe in Him; therefore, my prayers were spoken in haste and were without reverence and sincerity. In my mind, God stood between the mythical world and the world of reality. Why? Because it was all about me, just as we are taught by the world. I could only see myself because of my innate rationalization. I had taken care of myself since the age of sixteen. I worked my way up the corporate ladder. I bought the home for my family. I had security (money in the bank), and I did not see God in any part of my life. It was all about I and me, just as the world system would have it.

My wife was and still remains a Christian. She and some of her friends tried to talk to me on several occasions regarding God. But I did not want to hear of Him; after all, she was my wife, and I was doing the man thing for our home, not God. I did not see Him going to work every day, educating Himself in various skills to compete in the corporate world. I did not see Him bring home the paycheck. It was me that made all of those to come to pass again, so I believed.

I managed a department in a fast-growing company, and one of my subordinates was a Christian. One day, in my office, he shared part of his life with me. I in turn counseled him through the way of the world, and I shared his story with one of my peers. I also expressed my feelings of all Christians to him, which was "Christians are weak people who need something or someone to lay their heads on and cry to. They need to go and make something happen for themselves."

Well, that was when, I believe, God said enough is enough. It was not sixty days later when I was given the infamous pink slip. At that time, I thought the reason was based on the recent company acquisition but understanding later, it was God's way of teaching me and drawing me toward Him.

The lay-off did not concern me because my faith was in myself, and I was confident that I would find another position, one that was even better. My confidence in myself was so lofty I took thirty days before I would even consider upgrading my résumé. However, upon doing so, I made sure that it was the résumé of résumés, and I sent it out to all of the major companies. I received some responses, but the same responses left me unemployed.

I sent my résumé out again to other companies, not as well known. In the span of six months, I revised my résumé, toned it down, and sent it out, and again, nothing. I attempted to go into another profession, I tried going into business of my own, and I tried gas stations nothing, nothing and more nothing, nothing permanent. I was able to mow some lawns and shovel some sidewalks. I received odd jobs in plumbing, carpentry, painting, etc., but nothing substantial or consistent.

Through it all, God taught me that it was never about me, but it was all about Him. I could do nothing, nothing but fail, and as that became more and more apparent, I realized that it was God and always will be God, whoever He was.

Through this revelation, my spirit was made aware that God will have His way, and as He applied this understanding in my life, I started going to church with my wife. I knew of nothing else to do, and it was not as if I knew God or even if I wanted to know Him. The only thing that I did know for sure was I could not do anything on my own. I do understand that it was God's way of drawing me into the church and into His word.

I failed to mention that I was very analytical and had to break things down and rebuild them to thoroughly understand them. Therefore, when the church told me that I had to believe and I had to have faith, I did not understand and could not analyze it to understand it. Please keep in mind that up to this time in my life, I only knew that it was not about me or of me. I could no longer make anything happen; all doors were closed, and I still could not believe or have faith in anything or anyone, for who could help me if I could not help myself?

Unbeknownst to me, the Holy Spirit was working mightily in me. It was already seven months, and I still could not bring myself to believe or to have faith in anyone but myself, and I was still trying on my own even when I was going to church.

One day the Holy Spirit asked me if I knew God or if I knew of Him. That was easy and I said, thinking that I was talking to myself, "I know of Him."

It became crystal clear when the Holy Spirit made a statement in the way of a question when He asked me, "How can you have faith in, if you don't have knowledge of?" He then told me, "It is the *knowledge of* that produces *faith in*, which in turn, produces belief."

Even I understood that and subsequently picked up the Bible in the pursuit of knowing Him. As I studied and meditated on God's word, He has blessed me with the knowledge of Himself as well as faith and belief in Him, a balance that is so needed to endure the wiles of the enemy and to pursue the kingdom of God with boldness of heart.

Knowledge, faith, and belief are three of the ten factors of our spiritual balance and are part of the eight balances that the Christian should be aware of.

The Holy Spirit has quickened my spirit and led me to share with you "The Octagon of Spiritual Balances." My prayer is that you will receive as much of a blessing and spiritual understanding while reading this book as I have received in being the instrument used to write it.

CHAPTER 1

Spiritual Understanding

The term spiritual balance is used to help the Christian to visualize and understand the need of balance therefore enhancing and promoting stability and harmony between two or more factors in the Christian's life. As a result, a spiritual equilibrium is produced in the life of the Christian.

To construct a spiritual balance, there must be three or more factors involved. To prepare ourselves to receive this spiritual balance, we must first put our factors in order, that is, which one must precede, which one must follow, and which one must be used as the balancer.

Our first balance is comprised of faith, knowledge, and spiritual understanding. To receive the correct order and perspective, let us look at the word faith and begin by asking ourselves, what is faith and what does it mean? Take a moment before continuing to read and search your mind for your answer. Now let me tell you what faith is not. Faith is not reasoning, faith is not our intellect, faith is not our imagination, faith is not a thought, faith is not a feeling, faith is not a product of man, and faith is certainly not a sixth sense.

Faith

The substance and meaning of faith eludes most Christians, both laymen and clergy, because we are taught to believe that it is something in which we must perform and have control over. But truly, faith is a condition that we cannot perform under our own power. Our understanding of faith can only come from God. Therefore, we must rely on the word of God to tell us what faith is as well as its definition.

Hebrews 11:1 tells us, "Now faith is the substance of things hoped for, the evidence of things not seen." This is the only definition of faith we will find in the Bible, and to be honest, it does not do much for our understanding of the word or even the act of faith, and it does not help us to place it in the balance. Yet the enlightenment comes when we look at the verse with scrutiny.

In doing so, we come to realize that it is saying; faith is substance, and faith is evidence. Now, we must go to the original language to receive a greater understanding of the word faith.

In the Old English vernacular, faith is defined as substance and evidence. The same words in the Greek language are *hupostasis* (substance) and *elegehos* (evidence). Substance in the Greek is defined as to be confident, to have confidence, an assurance, and a guarantee. Evidence is defined as proof, a conviction. So it may be said that, faith is being sure of a certainty, or the confident assurance of something which is certain. We may even translate or paraphrase the scripture as now faith is the confidence of things hoped for, by the conviction of things not seen. Therefore, faith is the conviction of and confidence in something. It is a condition imparted within us, wherein we stand and endure until what is not seen comes to pass. It is a state of having conviction and confidence.

Now that we know what faith is, we must now place it in its appropriate order within our balance. To do that, we must first understand how we receive this conviction and confidence.

As the word of God explained what faith is, it will also tell us how we are to receive faith. However, we must first have a clear understanding of the meaning of the word faith. We know that faith is a conviction and confidence, but what does the word faith mean? *Pistis* is the Greek word for faith and is defined as a firm persuasion, to be persuaded.

So when we say that we have faith, it should mean that we are persuaded, and we are aware of that persuasion through our conviction and confidence of the same. This conviction and confidence can only come, can only stand the test of time, and can only endure to the end and withstand the ridicules of the world by one who is persuaded through an established and proven certainty. So faith is a conviction and confidence. The meaning or definition of faith is to be persuaded.

Faith is the substance; Faith is the evidence, the conviction and confidence, which are results of persuasion. We must be persuaded before the effects of faith are manifested inwardly. We must be persuaded before conviction sets in and before confidence responds to that conviction.

Let us remember that faith is not an emotional outburst, a thought, a feeling, our intellect, our imagination, and it is not a sixth sense. Faith is not reasoning, and it can't be analyzed, and if faith is not any of the aforementioned, then faith cannot come by these means.

Romans 10:17 tells us how we receive our faith, "Faith cometh by hearing, and hearing by the word of God." In "faith cometh by hearing," hearing is the process of persuasion, promoting conviction, and instilling confidence. As we are aware, our fore-parents Adam and Eve committed the first sin; therefore, we are born spiritually dead. However, our hearing or our spiritual ears are quickened and made alive as God draws us and produces the necessary work within us to start the process of "faith cometh by hearing."

Now this hearing is the "hearing by the word of God" and not the enticing words of man but rather hearing the word from God. Man may deliver the word of God, but we must hear the word from God. The same word is in John 1:1, "In the beginning was the word, and the word was with God, and the word was God." The Word, Jesus the Christ, and God are the same.

Before Jesus ascended to heaven, He left us this promise found in the Gospel of John 14 and 16.

> And I will pray the Father, and he shall give you another Comforter, that he may abide with you for ever; Even the Spirit of truth; whom the world cannot receive, because it seeth him not, neither knoweth him: but ye know him; for he dwel-

leth with you, and shall be in you. (John 14:16–17)

But the Comforter, which is the Holy Ghost, whom the Father will send in my name, he shall teach you all things, and bring all things to your remembrance, whatsoever I have said unto you. (John 14:26)

Howbeit when he, the spirit of truth come, he will guide you into all truth: for he shall not speak of himself but whatsoever he shall hear, that shall he speak: and he will shew you things to come. He shall glorify me: for he shall receive of mine, and shall shew it unto you. (John 16:13–14)

How do we receive our faith? It is by hearing God! Hearing the gospel from God as opposed to hearing the gospel of God from man starts God's process of faith, which is the process of persuasion, producing, and imparting conviction and confidence.

Faith does not come from the performance or elegant words of a speaker. Faith does not come from our feelings, emotions, intellect, or reasoning. Faith of God, in man, cannot be established by man. Faith comes from hearing personally and directly from God!

The word of the gospel spoken by man is good and is helpful. We are used by the Holy Spirit as vehicles and vessels to spread the gospel, but it is hearing God which imparts faith. It is God the Father, God the Son, and God the Holy Spirit who teaches us, guides us, persuades us, convicts us and instills within us that confidence which enables us to perform and to endure until the end. It is not self! It is not man! It is God!

We have come to the crucial point of understanding how we receive faith. It is imperative that we understand in order to construct and visualize this first spiritual balance. If the balance of faith is not properly received and placed, the stability and harmony in the Christian life will not exist. When stability and harmony is lacking in the life of the Christian, it affects the remaining seven of the octagon of spiritual balances therefore causing confusion, misunderstandings, and spiritual weakness.

I am not saying that we will not love God (as we understand love), but rather, our motives and actions will not be of the true faith of God if the balance of faith is not properly instituted by God within us.

Our faith is the corner stone of our spiritual life, as Jesus is the corner stone of the church. So it must be understood that, "Jesus is the author and finisher of our faith" (Hebrews 12:2). It is Jesus who plants our faith and increases it! It is not of ourselves! It is Jesus—the word through the comforter—the Holy Spirit! We must hear from God before we attempt to move in faith!

We must also realize that there are too many occasions in which we allow our emotions, thoughts, feelings, desires, and intellect to lead us as we attempt to affirm our position as faith in God. We even allow others to convince us, but we call it faith in God. There are times through reasoning, intellectual studies, and our overly active imaginations that we claim the results of such as having "received a word from God."

The Christian's desire for a particular person or thing can be overwhelming and so enticing that it too may lead the Christian to believe that pursuing a particular path or endeavor is the will of God in their life.

This is not the faith spoken of in the word of God. This kind of pseudo-faith may make you believe that you are walking a godly and spiritual life, but it is a ploy of the enemy and will fail you in the end.

That is why in 1 John 4:1, God warns us to "believe not every spirit, but try the spirits whether they are of God" We cannot serve God with a counterfeit faith. We cannot be obedient to God with a self-made faith. Our faith must come from God! God tells us in 2 Corinthians 13:5 to "examine yourselves, whether ye be in the faith; prove your own selves. Know ye not your own selves, how that Jesus Christ is in you, except ye be reprobates?"

God is telling us to test everything that comes in our hearts and minds via our thoughts or our senses and make certain they are from God. Our beliefs, actions, and posture of life are based on our faith. Therefore, we must hear God, and our faith must come from God if we are to obey Him.

We must examine and prove ourselves whether we are in the faith, which is of God and from God. If we are to have genuine faith in God, we must receive it from God! A counterfeit faith will fail us in the end!

The enemy is able, if we are not careful, to impart misleading information in our lives, which will affect our faith, and in our zeal we mistakenly accept it as coming from the Holy Spirit, and subsequently, it leads us unto destruction. We then become as those in Romans 10:2, those who "have a zeal of God, but not according to knowledge."

The enemy is subtle and very deceptive when it comes to our faith. He realizes that faith is the corner stone of the Christian's life, and if he can persuade us into believing a lie, he will distort our thoughts, motives, and actions therefore altering the Christian's life to one of discord and dissension, lacking stability and harmony.

So the Christian must be truthful, and ask, is what I believe is it of God or is it my imagination? Am I being deceived by the enemy? Is my love for a person, place, or thing leading me, or is it the will of God? Is this God's will or my desire? Are my beliefs and actions the results of reasoning, or am I truly hearing God? Is my life in accord with God, or am I doing what I would want God have me do? Am I aligned with His voice or is it my emotions? Am I hearing God, or am I following another unknowingly? Are my prayers according to His will? Do I have the zeal but lack the knowledge? We, the Christians, must understand that the only way we can obey God and perform His will is by faith. That is, hear Him and His will for us!

Romans 1:5 tells us that "we receive grace and apostleship, for the obedience to the faith." "For the obedience to the faith" means to obey that in which we have heard, to obey that in which we are sure of, to obey that in which we are persuaded of, and to obey what we have conviction of and what we have confidence in. Faith in God is to be persuaded by hearing from God. Remember Romans 10:17, "faith cometh by hearing, and hearing by the word of God."

Chapter 11 of Hebrews is called, by some, "the hall of faith." We receive a greater and fuller understanding of what faith is and how it works when we read this chapter, coupled with James 2:22 which states, "By works was faith made perfect?"

The word of God leads us to understand that the perfect faith God spoke of in the book of James consists of two phases. First we, like Noah and Abraham, must hear from God before we attempt to accomplish the work He has designated for us to do (see Hebrews 11:7–8). If we attempt to do the will of God prior to hearing from God, we are actually doing that in which we choose to do for God, and most likely, it is not in the will of God at all. Why? Because we acted on our own accord. Go back to the eleventh chapter of Hebrews. Did Noah build the ark before, or was it after he heard God express His will to him? Did Abraham leave his father's house to go into another country before, or was it after God expressed His will to him? The answer to these questions is after.

Yes, they of the ancient days and they who followed God first heard God before they moved to endeavor the will of God. The same is necessary today! Faith requires hearing from God first!

Hearing from God comes as quickly as a flash from a camera. It is a communication from the Holy Spirit to our spirits. Imagine a flash from a camera in the midst of our spirits. That is how fast the Holy Spirit is able to communicate His message.

However, the Holy Spirit imprints an understanding in our spirit of what God wants to make known to us. It is as quick as a flash; all of a sudden, we become aware without any input on or of our own, such as our senses, our thoughts, feelings, desires, or intellect. It is an understanding, a word from God, given by the Holy Spirit in our spirits!

After we have heard from God and if assurance is needed we "try the spirits whether they are of God" (1 John 4:1). We must now complete the second phase; if not, the first is dead.

The second phase is simply obeying the first phase. Otherwise, the Christian must first hear from God and then obey what he or she heard. True faith is what James called the perfect faith and that is first hearing from God then obeying. Yes, faith is hearing and obeying the word of and from God.

The two phases of faith are hearing and obeying. We cannot obey what we have not heard. If we attempt to obey anything but the voice of God, we are aligned with and partakers of what is evil. If it is not of the expressed will of God, then it is of the evil one! We are either obeying truth or error, the will of God or the will of Satan. There is no in between!

Should we hear the voice of God, expressing His will, and we do not obey. It becomes as James stated in James 2:26, "For as the body without the spirit is dead, so faith without works is dead also." "Faith made perfect?" is hearing God and obeying God. Again faith is all about God, and we must first hear Him then we must obey Him, and in doing so, our faith is made perfect.

Having the essential understanding of faith and its origin, which is, hearing and obeying God, being persuaded, having a conviction of and confidence in, all of which originates from and is imparted by God; we still cannot place faith in the balance without recognizing the order in which we are to receive it from God.

We will achieve the necessary comprehension in receiving faith as we discover the makeup of the two remaining factors, which are the two additional characteristics of the first spiritual balance.

Knowledge

To be persuaded, to have conviction, to be sure, and to have confidence, we must first have knowledge. In order to have any type of a relationship with anyone or anything, we must have some knowledge about them. To love, we must have knowledge of the person, place, or thing in which our love is demonstrated. Even in hate (as we should hate sin), we must have knowledge of it.

The knowledge of the world is obtained through our senses: our hearing, sight, smell, taste, and touch and is nurtured in the same manner by utilizing the same senses to justify and defend our thoughts, beliefs, and actions.

However, our spiritual knowledge is received through our spirit, and should indeed direct and control our knowledge of the world in order to justify and defend our spiritual walk. Therefore, our spiritual awareness and knowledge is understood to be the greater of the two, and they should not be thought of as the same. One will dominate the other!

This is where we fail to understand and distinguish the difference between our soul, which operates under the world's system and our spirit's spiritual awareness given by the Holy Spirit.

The knowledge of the world can be analyzed by the way and things of the world, but our spiritual awareness or knowledge cannot be explained in most cases, if at all except, that it comes from within, from God, and it is spiritual.

Our spiritual knowledge comes from God. This knowledge dwells within our spirit in God the Holy Spirit. This knowledge persuades and convicts. This knowledge causes us to perform in confidence and with boldness of heart. This same knowledge which persuades us is the inception of our faith, conviction, and confidence. This knowledge is spiritual knowledge, which is revealed spiritually and can only come from God!

We can understand the difference in our knowledge of the world and our spiritual knowledge as well as our soulish life and our spiritual life. But it becomes terribly difficult to discern between the two if we continue to focus on the things of the world. For example, we were aware of our physical birth and life before our spiritual birth. Yet we cannot live our spiritual life, that is, our new life based on our old life or on what our worldly senses attempt to persuade us as being the right thing to do.

The apostle Paul wrote to the Romans regarding the following concern of the old life and the new life:

> Brethren, my heart's desire and prayer to God for Israel is, that they might be saved. For I bear them record that they have a zeal of God, but not according to knowledge. For they being ignorant of God's righteousness, and going about to establish their own righteousness, have

> not submitted themselves unto
> the righteousness of God. For
> Christ is the end of the law for
> righteousness to everyone that
> believeth. (Romans 10:1–4)

Paul was referring to Israel, who like us was trying to achieve a new life by the means of the old one. They were attempting to acquire righteousness through the law as we try to live spiritually through our senses and the way of this world. Both have a zeal for God, "but not according to knowledge." Both strive to establish self-righteousness and in doing so, we are actually denying and rejecting the grace of God. As they did not submit to a new way of life and remained in the law, we do not submit to the spiritual way of life; instead, we remain in the physical.

The word knowledge found in Romans 10:2 is *epignosis* in the Greek language. It is derived from another Greek word *epiginosko* which means "to know fully, to become fully acquainted with in a complete sense, to have full knowledge of, to know intellectually." Now this type of knowledge is good and is obviously the knowledge possessed in Romans 10:2 by the way of the law. However, it is not the type of knowledge that is required to enable us to walk the Christian life.

The knowledge which we are to seek can only come from within our spirit, imparted by God the Holy Spirit. That knowledge is the Greek word *epignosis*, which is more intensive and expresses a more thorough participation first, of the Holy Spirit then of the Christian in its acquisition. It refers not only to the intellect but also a knowledge that powerfully influences the way and form of life, subsequently enhancing our Christian walk.

As faith, after persuasion, is the inner manifestation of the acceptance of divine revelation, knowledge is the comprehension of divine revelation and this knowledge must come before faith.

The Holy Spirit must first quicken our spirit, whereby our new birth is established and usher us into a spiritual awareness before we are able to develop spiritually.

As we must first be conceived in our new birth before we are able to walk the Christian life, we must first receive knowledge before we can have faith.

This was revealed to me by the Holy Spirit a number of years ago when He asked me, "How can you have faith if you don't have knowledge?" He then told me that "it is the knowledge that produces faith, which in turn produces belief."

Knowledge! That is influential knowledge, which draws the Christian closer to the Lord, knowledge which persuades, knowledge which convicts and imparts confidence, knowledge which instills spiritual boldness, an knowledge which comes from the depths of the Christian's spirit. Spiritual knowledge is that which dwells and works within us and through us. That is spiritual knowledge of faith.

Now that we understand knowledge must come before we can have faith; a balance can be constructed.

As I mentioned earlier, God uses the term spiritual balance to help the Christian to visualize and understand the need of balance also to enhance and promote stability and harmony between two or more factors in the Christian's life and as a result, it produces a spiritual equilibrium in the life of the Christian.

Stability and harmony are much-needed attributes in the Christian's life. Without them, there cannot be a balance between the Christian's thoughts, beliefs, and actions. There can only be confusion, misunderstandings, and spiritual weakness. Our love of God can be genuine, but our motives and actions will not be sincere or aligned with His will without the proper balance to create stability and harmony.

To construct a spiritual balance, there must be three or more factors involved. As I stated previously, our first balance is comprised of knowledge, faith, and spiritual understanding. Two are to be balanced, and one is to be the balancer. Understand that it is our knowledge and our faith which is in need of balance; therefore, spiritual understanding is the balancer of our knowledge and our faith.

Spiritual Understanding

If a Christian is to be righteous, the Christian's beliefs must be right. If the Christian's beliefs are to be right, the Christian's thoughts must be right. If the Christian's thoughts are to be right, the Christian must have an understanding which is balanced. Again, we are speaking of knowledge and faith being balanced but not with the extremities of our senses. If the Christian's knowledge and faith are to be balanced, it must be from within the Christian's spirit; therefore, the balance must result from having a spiritual understanding.

Our spiritual knowledge is received through our spirit; therefore, our spiritual understanding must also come from our spirit. If our knowledge is spiritual and our faith originates from our knowledge, our faith is spiritual as well. Should our knowledge and faith be spiritual and balanced by spiritual understanding, then our understanding must also be spiritual. If our understanding is spiritual and comes from within our spirit, then it can only come from God the Holy Spirit.

This is the point and place in which the Christian must turn and revisit throughout the Christian walk. The point is God! The place is in our spirit! We must seek God and His will within our spirit. We must hear God from within our spirit. This is where God the Holy Spirit resides. This is where He persuades and imparts conviction, confidence, and boldness of heart. This is where our knowledge and faith are received and balanced. God the Holy Spirit, who dwells within the Christian's spirit, is our spiritual understanding; therefore, He is also the balancer.

Now that God the Holy Spirit has been established as the beginning and balancer of all to come, we must again remember that spiritual understanding is not dependent on our feelings, emotions, thoughts, desires or intellect, and we cannot detect spiritual understanding through the gates of our senses; that is, our hearing, sight, smell, taste, or touch.

The apostle Paul prays in Colossians 1:9 that God's saints "might be filled with the knowledge of his will in all wisdom and spiritual understanding." He continues by telling us why in verse 10, "That you might walk worthy of the Lord unto all pleasing, being fruitful in every good work, and increasing in the knowledge of God; strengthened with all might, according to his glorious power, unto all patience and longsuffering with joyfulness."

God wants us to have knowledge of Himself and of His will. This knowledge is the same epignosis; which is not only of the intellect, but supports a more intensive thought involving a more thorough participation of the Holy Spirit and the Christian in acquiring knowledge. It is also the knowledge that very powerfully influences the Christian's life and walk. This knowledge comes by the way of the Holy Spirit, within the Christian's spirit as God's word is read and as His will is sought.

God tells us in Hosea 4:6, "My people are destroyed for the lack of knowledge: because thou hast rejected knowledge, I will also reject thee." If we continue to live the way of the world; in doing the things which we believe are right without hearing from God, we are thereby rejecting Him and His knowledge; therefore, He will reject us.

The Christian's initial responsibility is to seek God, His knowledge, and His will, and in doing so, God will reveal Himself. The Holy Spirit, our balancer of knowledge and faith, will also impart wisdom, spiritual understanding, conviction, confidence, and boldness in the heart of the Christian to perform the will of God our Father.

Knowledge of God's will and spiritual understanding fortifies the Christian's walk. The Christian will become fruitful, increase in knowledge, and will be strengthened "according to his glorious power." All which pleases God, God tells us in Isaiah 55:10–11:

> For as the rain cometh down,
> and the snow from heaven,

and returneth not thither, but
watereth the earth, and maketh
it bring forth and bud, that it
may give seed to the sower,
and bread to the eater: so shall
my word be that goeth forth
out of my mouth: it shall not
return unto me void, but it shall
accomplish that which I please,
and it shall prosper in the thing
whereto I sent it.

If the Holy Spirit dwells within us, God's word
also dwells within, and we can have a balance. But
should we lack balance, it may because we are not
seeking within our spirits.

As previously stated, our love of God can be
real, but our motives and actions will not be aligned
with God without the proper balance to create stability and harmony. If our understanding does not
come from our spirit, it is not spiritual, but it is carnal. If carnal, it cannot create a balance of stability
and harmony in our spiritual lives.

Since the initial sin of our fore-parents, Adam
and Eve, spirit and flesh have been contrary to each
other, and there is a constant and continuous battle
within the believer. God in Galatians 5:17 tells us,
"For the flesh lusteth against the Spirit, and the Spirit

against the flesh: and these are contrary the one to the other."

We must keep in mind that the enemy uses earthly things to deceive us. By developing a means of presentation the enemy arouses thoughts, feelings, desires, emotions, etc., in us in the name of the Lord, it causes us to believe that it is of the Lord. Again in 1 John 4:1, God warns us to "believe not every spirit, but try the spirits whether they are of God."

God is aware of the enemy's tactics and effectively warns us of the same. We, the Christians, must receive these warnings and apply them in our lives by testing the thoughts, feelings, desires, and emotions that can very easily overwhelm and beset us and discern if they are of God or not.

The enemy works from the outside going inward to subdue the Christian's spirit by enticing and deceiving the soul and body. The Holy Spirit works from within the Christian's spirit, instilling spiritual truth, spiritual awareness, encouragement, strength, and discipline to control the soul and then the body, outwardly. There is a constant battle going on for the life of the Christian. The ultimate battle is for control, but the method used by the spiritual forces involved is completely different and noteworthy. However, it is possible for us to distinguish between the two.

The rippling affect in a pond is clear evidence that something went in even without us actually seeing the cause of the ripple. Our discernment, through spiritual understanding of the work of God and the work of the enemy, is the same. If the Christian would truly and with spiritual sincerity adhere to the warning from God and test their thoughts, feelings, desires and emotions they would procure an understanding that God comes with peace, conviction, and confidence, he also comes without doubts, confusion, and ripples because He dwells within the spirit of the Christian. But on the contrary, the enemy is on the outside, trying to get in to oppress the spirit; therefore, causing ripples of doubt, confusion, weakness, and misunderstandings.

The enemy will even twist the word of God, taking it out of context to deceive us. Whatever he can use he will use as long as he can lead the Christian astray even unto destruction.

Remember Adam and Eve and what the enemy said to them about the word of God in Genesis 3:4–6:

> And the serpent said unto the woman, ye shall not surely die. For God doth know that in the day you eat thereof, then your eyes shall be opened, and ye shall be as gods, knowing good

and evil. And when the woman saw that the tree was good for food, and that it was pleasant to the eyes, and a tree to be desired to make one wise, she took of the fruit thereof, and did eat, and gave also unto her husband with her; and he did eat.

For the word of God to become real and powerful in the life of the Christian, it must be spiritually understood and practiced to repress the deceptive ways of the enemy. Without spiritual understanding, the enemy is able to make us feel that we believe without us actually believing. He is able to get us to the point where we do not know that we do not know.

Without spiritual understanding, the enemy can also prompt us to act on his will while believing it to be the will of God. The enemy's power of deceit comes from a lack of spiritual understanding and application within the Christian's life.

Spiritual understanding, originating from God the Holy Spirit, separates what is of God and from God from what is not; therefore, imparting the Christian with an awareness of spiritual truth. In turn, it initiates the balance of knowledge and faith, separating what is of spiritual truth and spiritual error as well as what is of the flesh and the natural instincts and desires.

We now understand that all knowledge should not be considered as coming from God and all what we believe does not always come from God because the enemy can influence us through our senses, our thoughts, feeling, desires, and emotions. The knowledge we possess has to be tested, purged, and refined before we hastily move, believing it is God speaking to us.

Before we move, we must seek for the truth and spiritual understanding of what is now known to us. We must ask, is it of God, and is it from God? If it is of God, the result will be the work of the Holy Spirit imparting conviction and confidence, which we refer to as faith.

James 2:21–22 tells us of the perfect faith "was not Abraham our father justified by works, when he had offered Isaac his son upon the altar? Seest thou how faith wrought with his works, and by works was faith made perfect?" Faith prompts our actions, but before we are to act, our knowledge and faith should be balanced by our spiritual understanding.

God, through the apostle Paul, told the Corinthians in 2 Corinthians 13:5 to "examine yourselves, whether ye be in the faith; prove your own selves." As I mention rather frequently in my little circle, "God's word still stands," therefore, we too need to examine ourselves before we step out on what we may believe is of God.

God's warning to us, to be spiritually balanced, should not be taken lightly. The deceptive schemes of the enemy will consume, mislead, and devour us should we not seek spiritual understanding.

This first balance cannot be overlooked. It is the beginning of the Christian's life and regeneration. If this balance is not properly arranged, all of the other factors and balances will be misleading. The Christian will also be confused, weak, unstable, inconsistent, uncertain, and unaware of their frail and depraved spiritual condition.

Our spiritual understanding quickens and imparts awareness in our spirit during our spiritual walk. It also promotes and balances our knowledge and our faith as well as our actions based on that knowledge. Therefore, the balancing factor of spiritual understanding must be revisited to ensure continuous spiritual stability and harmony throughout the octagon of spiritual balances.

CHAPTER 2

Knowledge

The second of the eight balances will also require three factors, and as we continue, we will become aware of how these factors are formatted in the balances. Two factors of the previous balance will remain, one of which taking on a new position, and one will be added.

As seen in the above scale, we now have knowledge as the balancer, and faith and belief are the two factors which require balance in the Christian's life. For a factor to become a balancer, it must first be balanced. The balancing of knowledge was accomplished with the faith factor in chapter 1. Knowledge must become a balancer prior to faith because faith cannot exist without knowledge; otherwise, faith comes from knowledge.

I stated in the previous chapter that God the Holy Spirit, who dwells within the Christian's spirit, is our spiritual understanding; therefore, He also is the balancer. From Him, we receive spiritual understanding of what is known to us. That, which is known, now becomes spiritual knowledge, and from this knowledge, faith is manifested in the spirit of the Christian. That is why it is essential for us to return to our spiritual understanding as well as revisit the balance of knowledge and faith to ensure spiritual guidance throughout our lives.

The manifestation of faith enables the Christian to believe, and in doing so, faith and belief are now part of the Christian's life. A true believer of Jesus cannot have one without the other. It is like the old cliché, "two sides of the same coin" and in this case, one being faith and the other belief. Spiritually speaking, we should have the proper spiritual understanding of what is known to us so that what we believe will be balanced with our faith.

We can ascertain a more comprehensible understanding if we go to the original language of the word of God. The Greek word for believe is *pisteuo*. It particularly means to be firmly persuaded toward something, to be assured, and to believe with the hope of certain expectations. The word pisteuo is also derived from another Greek word *pistis*, which in the English language translates into the word faith. We covered its definition and meaning in chapter 1; nonetheless, the need arises for a fresh recollection.

Faith is a firm persuasion and is also what is manifested in the believer, a conviction of and confidence in. When we have conviction and confidence we have faith, we are persuaded, and we believe what we have knowledge of.

We cannot have spiritual knowledge without spiritual understanding, and as previously mentioned, our spiritual understanding comes to us by the Holy Spirit, for He is our spiritual understanding. Therefore, it must be He who is to persuade us!

When we read the scriptures, it is the Holy Spirit who enlightens us to the truth. It is He who manifests faith in us and causes us to believe. The knowledge that is known by the Father, the Son, the Holy Spirit, and their teachings comes from the word of God. However, our spiritual knowledge and spiritual understanding come from the indwelling Holy Spirit and from persuasion.

What is being said here is, without persuasion we cannot have faith and without faith we cannot believe. This takes us back to the Greek definitions and derivatives of the words *pistis* (faith) and *pisteuo* (believe).

We come to understand that in the Greek language the word believe was derived from the word faith. So with the same understanding we know that we cannot have the word *pisteuo* (believe) if the word *pistis* (faith) did not exist. Accordingly, we cannot believe if we do not have faith. And faith comes by hearing, and hearing by the word of God. Otherwise, belief is derived from faith and faith comes from knowledge of and the persuasive work of the indwelling Holy Spirit.

What we have is the evident work of the Holy Spirit. He is the one who will persuade, convict, impart confidence, and assure us that all we receive from Him through the word of God; by Him, is truth. Our concern at this point should be that of self and the work of the enemy. We should not allow our overly active imagination to become prominent, attempting to conjure up a false word or understanding based on our human emotions.

This is where most Christians experience defeat and failure. This false word or false understanding produces false hope, and their anticipated outcome falls short in regard to what was expected. When this happens, the Christian usually does not express the unanswered, self-inflicted prophecy. They drown it in their sorrow, never to be disturbed again, except on those occasions when they reflect, in wonder, as to why a certain expectation did not come to pass.

There are others who will state simply that it was "not the will of God," but neither one will concede to their error in faith. Therefore, they allow the enemy to continue to distort and sabotage the manner in which they believe.

The Christian's principle of belief is through faith, knowledge, and spiritual understanding. When we allow the enemy to come in and distort the message of God by imparting and mixing our desires, thoughts, emotions, intellect, and self-will with the word of God, we fall short every time. Then, it is no longer the will of God or faith in God that leads us. It is now our will and our desire we claim in the name of God, even unconsciously.

That is the life pattern of most Christians, and many accuse the outcome on their lack of faith. What we must understand is, it was not true faith in or from God. Their belief was misappropriated based on false or misleading information, resulting in their expectation not being manifested. The faith that they relied on did not come from God, for if it did, it would have come to pass! We need to tell our brothers and sisters just that so they will start to "try the spirits to see whether they are of God" (1 John 4:1).

Remember, "faith cometh by hearing, and hearing by the word of God" (Romans 10:17). Faith starts with hearing spiritually from God. And that, which was spiritually heard will come to pass! Why? In Isaiah 55:11, God tells us, "So shall my word be that goeth forth out of my mouth: it shall not return unto me void, but it shall accomplish what I please, and it shall prosper in the thing whereto I sent it."

Our faith becomes imbalanced when our belief is motivated by something other than God's unction. There are many Christians today who believe that they will be financially prosperous and put all of their efforts toward that belief. Their belief is not based on the word of God, and they did not hear it from God but solely on preaching false prophecy and the twisting of scripture by man.

There are other Christians who were convinced that they were healed from a sickness or disease only to find out in time that it was not the truth. Rather than questioning the origin of their belief, they drown in their sorrow or assess that it was not God's will for their healing.

We, as Christians, must stop listening to man's plan and turn to God. We must see man as who he is and God as who He is. There are times when I truly believe that man is trying to work God instead of allowing God to work in and through him.

When Christ died on the cross, the veil in the temple was rent in two. This remains a symbolic sign to man that no longer is there a need of an intercessor to approach God on our behalf. Man, without the knowledge of God, will lead us into destruction. But the word of God will accomplish what pleases Him and prosper in the things where He sent it. So it is imperative that the Christian will seek to hear directly from God!

Our spiritual knowledge will balance our faith and our belief to discern truth from error. That knowledge comes from the word of God, the hearing of His voice and our spiritual understanding, which is the Holy Spirit persuading us and supporting the truth of God.

There are far too many Christians who believe that they are performing the will of God. Their attempts to do God's will is based on what they think they know of God. In most cases, the individuals have not read the word to know the will of God; therefore, it leaves them incapable of performing according to God's direction.

They rely on pastors, preachers, teachers, or anyone else who appears to be exalted in the body of Christ. It is sad but true that those who do rely on others have not read the word of God for themselves or have not received spiritual understanding directly from God. They are unable to effectively discern truth from error. They put their faith, and consequently, the outcome of their belief in the hands of those who claim to be someone of importance in the body of Christ. Otherwise, their faith and belief are in what man tells them and not in God.

God warns us in 2 Corinthians 11:13–15 that "for such are false apostles, deceitful workers, transforming themselves into the apostles of Christ. And no marvel; for Satan himself is transformed into an angel of light. Therefore it is no great thing if his ministers also be transformed as the ministers of righteousness."

Yes, God does use man as a vehicle to spread the gospel, but we need to know if the person proclaiming the word of God is proclaiming it in truth before we accept it. Our responsibility is to seek spiritual knowledge to balance our faith and belief.

If we do not possess true knowledge of the word of God, we will not have a balancer of our faith and belief. As an act of faith if we do not have knowledge of the word of God, then we must ask ourselves where did our faith come from, and who or what is our faith in? True faith in God can only come from God and His word. Faith which comes any other way is deceptive and counterfeit.

Most Christians, both lay and clergy, have been adhering to a type of false faith for most of their Christian lives. Because they are not sufficient in the word and the knowledge that is required by God, they continue to lack spiritual stability and harmony. Therefore, they fluctuate and remain spiritually weak.

Remember Paul's desire for the saints of God in Colossians 1:9 that God's saints, "might be filled with the knowledge of his will in all wisdom and spiritual understanding." When we lack spiritual knowledge, our fallen nature is in control, and mixed with our zeal for God, Satan will present a false faith. Like those in Romans 10:2, "they have a zeal of God, but not according to knowledge. For they being ignorant of God's righteousness, and going about to establish their own righteousness have not submitted themselves unto the righteousness of God." It is time for us to reject Satan's deceptive representation of faith and restore the validity of God's word. We must seek the truth, righteousness, and spiritual knowledge, which is required to produce and balance true faith and belief.

The lack of knowledge will give Satan a foothold, allowing him to mislead us by accruing and applying a message or false doctrine within us and instilling a belief which lacks in substance and truth. This false belief is then nurtured through the eloquence of speech, the tickling of the ears, and through preaching and teachings that feed our emotions. A false message will also accommodate those who tend to choose what they want to hear. Subsequently, hearts and minds receive the message as coming from God when in truth, it does not.

They think their faith is in God, but their belief comes from another spiritual source, causing: confusion, disharmony, spiritual weakness, instability. and gross spiritual imbalance.

When our faith and our belief are unbalanced, we actually believe what we really have no faith in. We believe in what we are not really certain of. We believe in what seems right, feels right, or what we desire to be right. Therefore, our faith is now altered by the wiles of satanic influence, unbeknownst to the believer.

Our belief implants trust and guides us through life, therefore if we are to be led spiritually by the Holy Spirit; our belief must come from our faith in God, which in turn, comes from our knowledge of God, derived from our spiritual understanding of God's word and His will for our lives. Our faith and our belief must be balanced by our knowledge, which is governed by our spiritual understanding, the Holy Spirit.

Again the Christian must be truthful and ask, is that what I believe of God, or is it my imagination? Am I being deceived by the enemy? Is it God's will or my desire? Are my beliefs the results of reasoning, or am I actually hearing God? Is my life in right accord with God, or am I doing what I want God to have me to do? Am I aligned with His voice or my emotions? Am I hearing God, or am I following another unknowingly? We must be certain that our belief originates from our faith in, of, and from God!

If we allow Satan or ourselves anywhere in the structure of the balances, we will be putting our spiritual walk and life in jeopardy. We must have clarity of mind and discernment of the unction by the Holy Spirit. We must also know enough about Satan and ourselves to be able to discern the difference.

If we leave our desires and preconceived thoughts behind and seek the truth by reading and studying the word of God, the balances will be erected by the Holy Spirit, and Satan and ourselves will be abandoned!

If we have gained knowledge and the application of the word of God is balanced by our spiritual understanding, then our belief will respond only to that faith and persuasion. What we have conviction of will elevate us to the level of spiritual trust.

CHAPTER 3

Faith

We are told by God in Proverbs 3:5–6 to "Trust in the Lord with all thine heart; and lean not unto thine own understanding. In all thy ways acknowledge him, and he shall direct thy paths."

In the third balance, faith balances our belief and trust. Of these three factors, one cannot exist in the life of the Christian without the other. They are so closely tied that the word faith can be used inclusively for this trio.

The Hebrew word for trust is *batach*; its meaning is to attach oneself, to trust, to confide in, feel safe, be confident, secure, to be careless. It is a confident expectation.

The enemy is very much aware of the arrangement and significance of the spiritual balances; therefore, he has an advantage and is able to distort the factors within the balances. For example, if our spiritual understanding is in error, every factor of the octagon of spiritual balances will be unbalanced, and the Christian's life will be one of discord, misunderstandings, confusion, weakness, and spiritual depravation.

When our spiritual understanding, knowledge, and faith are balanced but our belief does not originate from our faith, our trust will not be aligned with our faith, knowledge, and spiritual understanding. We are therefore confined on a constant spiritual roller coaster, unknowingly lacking true spiritual understanding of belief and trust.

Unfortunately, there are many Christians today who are in that situation. No one can tell them that they are enveloped within the deceptive will of Satan. They will physically oppose you before you will convince them of the deceit they have fallen prey to. This is how powerful Satan's lies can be, once embraced as belief.

Should we discern this in another brother or sister, address it openly and in love. But if we are rebuked, we should continue to keep them in our prayers. We should likewise examine ourselves and determine if we are receptive to personal reproof. Do we have an open mind to the word of God? Do we believe every word of the Bible and apply His word in our lives, or are our minds closed and veiled by the deception of the enemy? He is subtle and very cunning. He can be controlling the life of a person, claiming to be the son or daughter of God without him or her realizing it. We must compare what we trust, believe, and have faith in with the actual word of God.

This may possibly be the time to look at ourselves and judge where we stand. Be truthful and honest; ask yourself, is what I believe of God, or is it my imagination? Am I being deceived by the enemy? Is my love for a person, place, or thing leading me, or am I led by the expressed will of God? Is this my desire? Are my beliefs and actions the results of reasoning, or am I hearing God? Is my life in accord with God, or am I doing what I would want God to have me to do? Am I aligned with His voice or my emotions? Am I hearing God, or am I following another, unknowingly? Are my prayers according to His will? Do I have the zeal but lack the knowledge? Do I feel safe? Do I have a confident expectation? Do I truly trust Him?

These are tough questions to ask yourself, but the toughest thing is answering the question honestly. Secondly, we have to take the corrective measurement(s) to overcome what we may have been doing incorrectly all of our Christian lives. We cannot allow our pride to keep us in bondage and prevent us from reaching that balance of spiritual equilibrium.

We must first understand and then confess that we are in error, repent, and ask God for His forgiveness, and that deceptive hold that the devil had will be broken! Reconstruction of the balance or balances can take place by the Holy Spirit.

As stated, trust is having a confident expectation, feeling safe, and being secure. This trust comes from our belief which is derived from our faith. Trust must be built upon both belief and faith, with knowledge of and spiritual understanding as its foundation.

When God told us in, Proverbs 3:5–6 to "trust in the Lord with all thine heart; and lean not unto thine own understanding. In all thy ways acknowledge him, and he shall direct thy paths," God is telling us we are to leave our fleshly way of understanding behind. When we acknowledge Him, we believe and we know without a doubt everything is going to work for the good. This pleases Him!

God is sovereign. He controls all things. He causes, allows, or disallows. Nothing can be done without the knowledge of God prior to its manifestation. If God causes it, allows it, or disallows it, it will work for His good purpose. God tells us in Romans 8:28 that "all things work together for good to them that love God, to them who are the called according to his purpose." With that understanding, we should be ready to praise Him even before the outcome is realized.

King David, in Psalm 56:3–4 said unto God, "What time I am afraid, I will trust in thee. In God I will praise his word, in God I have put my trust." Our concerns should not involve how or when God is going to operate on our behalf. If our thoughts are constantly on what is to be accomplished, we can say that our trust has not yet reached its spiritual maturity.

Trusting in God is giving all up to God, knowing that in His time and in His way it will be as He chooses it to be. God tells us in Isaiah 55:8, "For my thoughts are not your thoughts, neither are your ways my ways." If we are equipped with what is needed to trust God, and to be fully secure with a confident expectation, we will be ready to accept what He chooses to give or to remove as we put our cares in His hands and continue to do His work with clarity of mind until He brings about fruition.

Our concern should be, at this point, do we truly trust in God? Can I give all to God to do as He chooses: my house, my transportation(s), my job, my boat, my bank account, my land, and my business for Him to maintain, to build, or to take away at His will? Can I surrender my life to Him, my wife's life, my sons and daughters, grandchildren, friends, other family members, and relatives? Can I give all that I have? Can I give my all? Can I truly give it to God and trust Him to perform His will in His way for my own good?

Job, in Job 13:15 stated, "Though he slay me, yet I will trust in him." Do we have the same spiritual understanding and fortitude as Job? Can we be as certain as Abraham was when God told him to render his only son for a sacrifice?

We have many Christians who will confess that they are able to give all to God, but the truth is not in them. If our hearts and minds remain focused on what we gave up to God, we did not surrender it to Him. Once we surrender all to God, our mind should be clear. We should feel safe knowing the situation is then in the hands of God. Our acceptance or consciousness may remain, but the outcome should not concern us any longer.

Soon after Judah was taken into captivity by the Babylonians, they were told to bow down and worship an image. There were three Hebrew boys known in the Persian tongue as Shadrach, Meshach, and Abednego. When the decree came to bow to this image, their refusal to perform this commandment exemplified the greatest trust in God's ability that man can display. They said to the king in Daniel 3:16–18:

> O Nebuchadnezzar full of fury,
> we are not careful to answer

thee in this matter. If it be so, our God whom we serve is able to deliver us from the burning fiery furnace, and he will deliver us out of thine hand, O king. but if not, let it known unto thee, O king, that we will not serve thy gods, nor worship the golden image which thou has set up.

This is not a fly-by-night trust! This is not a superficial trust! This is not a trust that can be conjured by man, and this is not a lip service trust. This trust cannot be instilled by or performed in the strength of man. This trust must overcome the fallen nature and defeat that screams from the soulish life of the world. This trust must capture the heart, mind, and soul. This is a spiritual trust!

This trust can only be imparted spiritually! This trust can only be understood spiritually! This trust must come through the spirit of the Christian. This trust breaks the bond, lies, and desires of Satan, the soul and the flesh. This trust comes from a balanced belief, faith, knowledge, and spiritual understanding.

Our faith and our belief evolve from the fact that God is able to do anything, and He will do what pleases Him. Our trust should be based on the same criterion. But as soon as our trust starts to distort what God has spoken and believe that He will do for us exactly as He did or was doing for others, we lose the perspective of our faith.

Remember, in Romans 10:17, "Faith cometh by hearing, and hearing by the word of God." As our faith and belief is in what we hear from God, so too should our trust. We should not trust that God will act on our behalf in the same manner as any other individual. We should trust that God will do what He has expressly revealed to our spirit.

There are those who trust that God will give them financial prosperity because He gave to another. They are taught and believe in a false doctrine that all of God's children are to be financially wealthy. There are also those who believe that God will heal them because He healed another, or they are taught and believe in a false doctrine that none of God's children should be sick or diseased.

Our trust should not be based upon the doctrine of man. Our trust must be in what we personally hear from God concerning His will in and for our lives. My trust is in what God tells me! My belief is in what God has made known to me! My faith is in what God convinces me of and His imparted confidence.

Our understanding of spiritual trust must be determined from the previous balanced factors. We must refer to prior factors and balances to ensure that we are hearing and adhering to the voice of God. Should our trust be balanced with our spiritual belief, it will then escalate us to the next level of spiritual balance.

Should our false trust continue to disappoint us by not manifesting desired results, the previous balances will soon diminish. If we can no longer trust in what we believe will come to pass, how can we continue to have faith in what we have knowledge of? If our trust is destroyed, every other factor will go with it, and we will be positioned exactly where the enemy will have us be, believing and trusting only in ourselves and worldly tangibles.

There are many Christians in this situation. They do not address their failures or examine those things which they based their trust on to come to pass. The truth of the matter is, they did not hear it directly from God.

Our trust must be balanced with what we believe by our faith based on what we heard directly from God. Should we hear from God and then take action, it develops what James calls in James 2:22, the perfect faith, and what we trust to take place will come to pass.

CHAPTER 4

Belief

As the comprehension of trust permeates our spirits, great hope is produced and cascades within our hearts and minds. Our fourth balance will consist of trust, hope, and belief. Hope will be added with trust, and subsequently, both will be balanced by belief.

Hope is a word which is read and used but not completely understood by most Christians. Its spiritual meaning and strength are all too often unrealized. Therefore, it remains obscure, and the result of its usage is reduced to the method, in which man perceives hope, and the flesh takes control of what should be spiritual.

The mind of man perceives and defines hope as the feeling of what is desired and is attainable, or a possibility that the events may turn out for the best. Man will say, "If I truly hope with certainty, I will receive." This hope is brought on by the enemy through the flesh and is a false hope. This perception of hope can turn in any direction; otherwise, it may or may not come to pass.

This type of hope can be used to motivate, to manipulate, and to inflict pain for self-gain. This hope, in most cases, is used by the Christian who believe that he or she is doing what is best, but it is still based on a feeling, a desire, or the possibility that the outcome will be what one longs for.

When the flesh moves us into the arena of hope, it brings us unknowingly in the realm of uncertainty. I say in the realm of uncertainty because the flesh does not know what is going to take place in the future. It can only hope as it defines hope as a possibility. If there is a possibility, then there is a place for false hope or the probability of chance. This is not the hope which the Bible refers to. What we do in the flesh is called the probability of chance. We understand that it can only go one way or the other, so we opt to hope for what we desire.

If we are honest with ourselves, we will admit that what we hoped for may not turn out the way we have chosen. But in doing so, we have defeated the hope within, so we will not acknowledge what has just as much of a possibility to happen.

In truth, we are not sure of what is going to take place so we lean on the probability of chance in the name of the Lord. We say in the name of the Lord because "God is able." We know that God is able; yet, we still allow the flesh to impart uncertainty in our hearts and minds and claim it in the Lord's name. Again in most cases, this is done unknowingly by the believer.

When we claim anything in the name of the Lord, it seems as if we are seeking for some type of empowerment for our hope to manipulate the outcome. This uncertainty is not of God or is it from God. This uncertainty cannot maintain the spiritual balance in a believer's life. A manipulated outcome cannot balance a child of God.

As our knowledge, faith, belief, and trust come to us spiritually through our spirits, we must also receive our hope spiritually. Should hope develop by any other means, it is not of God, and the outcome will always be uncertain. However, should our hope come from God, it will impart certainty and confidence. Let us revisit some of the factors that have been previously balanced. Knowledge comes from the word of God and is used to persuade us. Faith is an attribute one has when he or she has been persuaded, received confidence, and have conviction. Belief is very much the same as faith; if you have faith, you also believe in what you have faith in. Otherwise, you believe in what you have been persuaded of. It is two sides of the same coin. Trust is a confident expectation and can only come from one's belief.

This now brings us to hope. Hope, when it is of and from God, is a confident expectation, a conviction, and an assurance. Hope is having an explicit and certain understanding of what is to come. Hope is knowing what God has imparted will come to pass. It is all about our knowledge of God and what God persuades us of.

Hope is yoked with trust, and both are balanced by our spiritual belief. It is what we believe in or what we are persuaded of that balances trust and hope. Should our belief produce a trust that is false, our hope will be uncertain from its conception. But if all factors are balanced, our hope will come from Him whom we trust, believe, have faith in, and know of. This is certain hope and will come to pass.

The apostle Paul wrote in Titus 1:2 that he was "in hope of eternal life." Should we view this hope as we understand it in the flesh and not based on what God has persuaded him of, we can only surmise Paul's hope as one of uncertainty and his desire and longing for eternal life as a possibility.

But Paul also mentioned in the same verse regarding the hope of eternal life, "which God, that cannot lie, promised before the world began." In this, we can see several things of God and of Paul. First,

Paul said that God cannot lie, and this can only mean that Paul had to know God personally to possess this knowledge. Secondly, Paul said what God had promised, which surely testifies that Paul had heard directly from God and was persuaded. This also underscores the beginning of our spiritual balance. It is through knowledge that the Holy Spirit persuades us, and this persuasion imparts faith, belief, trust, and hope.

We must always remember that it is through our spirits we are able to acknowledge the truth. It is through our spirits that we receive the message of God. It is through our spirits that we are able to receive faith. It is through our spirits that we are able to believe. It is through our spirits that we are able to trust God. And it is through our spirits that hope is manifested.

In Romans 15:13, we find these words written by the apostle Paul, "Now the God of hope fill you with all joy and peace in believing, that ye may abound in hope, through the power of the Holy Ghost." What Paul is saying is God is the source of our hope, and we prevail in hope through the power of the Holy Spirit.

Hope is given to us when we trust in God. Without trust, how can one have hope? Without belief, how can we trust? Without faith, how can we believe? Without knowledge, how can we have faith? Without spiritual understanding, how can we acknowledge the truth?

God is our hope, and He dwells within us. He is empowering our faith, belief, trust, and hope. It is not of us! Our hope is not based on the uncertainty of our desires, needs, or our feelings. However, should we base our hope on what God promises, we will receive the promise or something greater.

A balanced believer recognizes that if he or she does not receive hope by hearing God, then that hope is only a possibility and is uncertain. Yet if we hear God speaking to us, in the way that He does, in a flash, it instills certainty and confident expectation upon conception.

Paul's hope for eternal life was not one of uncertainty but one of assurance. He knew without a doubt the certainty of his eternal life because he heard it from God.

God also tells us in 1 John 5:13, "These things have I written unto you that believe on the name of the son of God; that you may know that you have eternal life." Through the knowledge of the word of God along with a balanced faith, belief, and trust, hope is imparted and assured. Hope becomes so certain and absolute that it enables us to move to the next level of the octagon of spiritual balances.

CHAPTER 5

Trust

After our hope is secured, God's love for us becomes so inviting that it creates a spiritually captivating appeal, and its attractiveness promotes spiritual excitement and motivation in the life of the believer.

It is as if a door was opened and a light so brilliant yet so clear, shone on us and imparted a love that cannot be denied physically or spiritually. It is a love for God, a love for His will and His way, and a love that can only be thoroughly understood experientially. It is a love that changes our lives completely and intimately. It awakens us to a realm we had no idea existed and promotes a new way of life.

Prior to this, we did have a longing for God and His word as He drew us to Him. But it seems as if it is at this time our desire is to be with Him all of the time, the closer the better as our will conforms to His will.

Maybe it is because the previous balances are stable. Yes, that must be it! It could be nothing else! I now have a love that abides within and has displaced the love of the world yet one that now thirsts to be shared with the world.

I even have hope of eternal life. My trust in Jesus, even unto death, is a trust that cannot be compared to any other person, place, or thing. My belief in God and His word is without question. My faith is constantly abounding. As I continue to read and study the word of God, my knowledge of Him continues to increase, and in doing so, my spiritual understanding is being fulfilled. It must be because the previous balances are stable.

This love from God cannot be fully realized with a previous imbalanced factor. Our knowledge of God the Father, God the Son, God the Holy Spirit, and the teachings of the word must be sufficient, and our faith, belief, trust, and hope must be balanced and in order.

Love should be utilized as a major checkpoint in the believer's life. If that light has not yet shone on you, if love for God, His will, and His way is not the utmost in your life, and if love does not have a thirst to be shared with others, then it is not the type of love one should seek after or be content with.

The love that God gives and desires for us comes from within our spirit, and it can only be manifested through the spiritual understanding of God and His word, which is the source of the light, previously mentioned.

The love that God gives is an unselfish love—impartial, sincere, fervent, and abounding. It is a divine love so it is unchanging, self-sacrificing, inseparable, and constraining.

It is the same love that Jesus had and commands us to have in John 15:12 when He told us, "This is my commandment, That you love one another, as I have loved you." If He commanded us to love as He has loved, then this love is attainable for the believer.

If we do not have this love, then there is an imbalance in our lives, and that imbalance can come from any one of the previous balances or factors. The same imbalance obviously prevents us from experiencing the love which Jesus had, and what we do express as love is according to the way of the world a soulish love.

Love of the world, the soulish love, is a selfish love, a love that covets. The love of the world will not bear the burdens of others. The love of the world will exploit the weak and ignorant. The love of the world is fervent only for self. It is partial and evil. This love is an envious and jealous love because it bites whenever another, even seemingly, profits. It does not want others to be accomplished. This love loves only for its desires and gains. Never for the needs or wants of others!

The love of the world will attempt to justify itself. However, within the believer's spirit he or she knows that there is no justification only an imbalance in life.

As previously stated, the love from God comes from within the spirit of man and cannot be substituted. When the believer receives this love, it will manifest in the spirit of the believer, a spiritual understanding of the will and way of God and cannot be forged by any other power.

Once this has taken place, the believer can never be deceived by love again because the difference is so distinct, as distinct as light and darkness and is recognized by the believer. However, the use of this love must be governed, for an overly zealous love can lead us to places and people outside of the will of God and cause us to perform what is not in the will of God. But we will address this principle in the next balance.

God tells us in 1 John 4:16, "God is love; and he that dwelleth in love dwelleth in God, and God in him." He also tells us in verse 19 and 20, "We love him, because he first loved us," and "If a man say, I love God, and hateth his brother, he is a liar: for he that loveth not his brother whom he has seen, how can he love God whom he has not seen?" Now that is a statement and a question that should receive our undivided attention. First, we love Him only because He loved us first. God initiates our love for Him, and His love must be imparted in us for us to love Him. This is done by receiving the light through our balanced hope and trust and the spiritual understanding of God and His word. Without spiritual understanding, spiritual love cannot thrive in our lives.

Secondly, if we claim to love God and we have a disdain or hate for another even our enemy, there is no truth in what we claim. This is the word of God, not mine. Please do not rebuke the word of God by saying, "Yes, I hate, but I still love God. If you can justify such a statement, you are saying God is a liar; that is, we can hate one another and love God simultaneously.

We must come to understand that there is an imbalance and seek to correct ourselves and not the word of God. As far as loving our enemy, God tells us in Matthew 5:43–48, "Ye have heard that it hath been said, Thou shalt love thy neighbor, and hate thine enemy. But I say unto you, Love your enemies, bless them that curse you, do good to them that hate you, and pray for them which despitefully use you, and persecute you."

Jesus tells us in John 14:15, "If you love me, keep my commandments." If there is a problem or a concern with who we can or cannot love, it will originate with us, not with the word of God.

I realize that it is hard to confess, especially to ourselves, when we are in error. However, our trust in and desire to love God should enhance our strength to do so. Without a confession, we will remain as we are and additional spiritual growth will not be possible.

We will remain unstable, confused, vulnerable, and spiritually weak. More importantly, Satan will continue to have control. Should this happen, then we may not be who we profess to be! The love that God desires for us to have and to share with others, even our enemies, is what is known in the Greek language as *agapé* (ag-ah´-pay). Its meaning is an affectionate regard, goodwill, and benevolence. This is also an unconditional love! It is to be given without merit and respect for person. It is a love of good will toward others, the love of a neighbor, a brotherly or sisterly affection.

You may say that does not seem to be a very difficult thing to perform. Then I ask, why is it not being done? Why cannot most husbands love their wives in the manner that God stated, "Husbands feel agape for your wives." Why cannot most wives love their husbands in the same manner? Our problem in most cases is we find ourselves not in love with our spouse. So we stop caring.

I knew a person some years ago, and during one of our conversations, he told me that he was going to divorce his wife. Right away, I expressed my sorrow for her adultery during their marriage. He in turn and very adamantly stated that I was in error and that she had never cheated on him. I asked without hesitation, "Why then are you divorcing her when God has said divorce is only sanctioned in proven cases of adultery?"

He pushed that aside very quickly as he rebuked me by saying he serves a forgiving God. However, the reason he confessed about divorcing his wife was, and I quote, "I am not in love with her any longer."

I will tell you as I told him, "God did not tell us to be in love with our spouse. He said to feel agape for our spouse, to care for, do for, to show concern for, and to be affectionate toward her is the expressed love that God refers to." Yes, it would be easier if we were in love with our spouse, but God did not command us to be in love, but to feel agape. Do you have agape for your spouse or has your marriage become a living convenience? Do you claim to love God? If so, you must have agape for your spouse.

Pastors, do you feel agape for those who God has sent to you or has it become a job, a way to receive an income? Are you seeking their spiritual welfare or are you just preaching on Sundays? You cannot feel agape for them at a distance! You cannot have agape for them without knowing them!

If we do not receive the love that God desires for us to have for others, how can we say that we love God? How can God perform what pleases Him if His love does not exist within those who claim Him as Lord?

We must revisit the previous balances and correct what is preventing God's love from manifesting into our lives. We need to separate ourselves from our worldly emotions, feelings, desires, fears, and thoughts. Put Satan in check; balance what is not balanced and receive that light, the love that God has for us. This will change our emotions, feelings, desires, fears, and thoughts therefore providing us what we need to further our spiritual growth.

When we receive that love, Jesus tells us in John 15:9 to "continue ye in my love." Love is just that precious to the Lord. Not only does He want us to receive it, but also continue in it and to walk in it.

Love is the ultimate and that is why we must love and use it as a major check point. I say love is the ultimate because "God is love." If we do not have the light to see, which is the love from God in us, we do not have God!

God, through the author of the book of 1 Corinthians, tells us in 1 Corinthians 13:13, "Now abideth faith, hope and charity, these three but the greatest of these is charity." The Old English word charity is our English word love and would read as "now abides faith, hope and love… but the greatest of these is love." Why is love being pressed on us, and why is love the greatest of them all?

Let us look at faith, hope, and love with a heavenly view. First, faith will not be needed in heaven by virtue of the fact that He whom we had confidence in and had conviction of will be seen in heaven. Secondly, hope will be of no concern since we will then have all that is essential to live in heaven. We will be living that faith as well as what we hoped for.

Ultimately, both faith and hope will be fulfilled and realized, and we will be living in perfection without a need throughout eternity. However, our love will continue for eternity with the greatest love of all, God. So love is impressed upon us on Earth to enable us to understand the will of God as we execute the definition and character of God in the world.

In heaven, the need for love is apparent. If God is love, we need to achieve closely a simulation of love as possible. Although God is going to assure the believer's love, the octagon of spiritual balances will enhance our understanding as God draws us and make us the servants of His choice.

CHAPTER 6

Love   *Obedience*

Hope

Let us review the previous balances we have discovered. The first balance is faith and knowledge balanced by spiritual understanding. The second balance is faith and belief balanced by knowledge. The third is belief and trust balanced by faith. The fourth is trust and hope balanced by belief. The fifth is hope and love balanced by trust. We can now approach the next spiritual balance for continual development and enhancement of our spiritual equilibrium and awareness.

This sixth balance presents our love and obedience balanced by godly hope. Within this balance, our spiritual stability will become profound, both in us and toward those who share our lives. This, too, is where our spiritual understanding and other previous balances are revisited to reaffirm the truth. This is where our knowledge of God and his word proves harmonious on our behalf.

For example, God's warning to us is that there are evil spirits who have deceived prophets and teachers from the beginning of time, and Satan is their father. Therefore, we are not to believe everything that we hear.

The evil spirits that deceived believers in the ancient times are the same spirits that attempt to deceive us in this present day by instilling erroneous thoughts and beliefs in us. How these spirits are able to inject lies and false doctrines in our hearts and minds is unknown, but they are capable of doing so!

Obeying the word of God either from written form or from the Holy Spirit through our spirits initiates the manifestation of the will of God in the life of the believer. This is where, as they say, "The rubber meets the road."

As James said in James 2:26, "For as the body without the spirit is dead, so faith without works is dead also." This was covered in chapter 1. James also said in James 2:22 that "by works was faith made perfect." Obedience is that work! Remember the two phases of faith. First, the believer hears from God. Second, we must obey what we heard. However, as we are eager to make that step of obedience, we must first be certain that we heard from God. We must be sure that it is God whom we are obeying and not the enemy unknowingly.

We can have a boundless zeal to do the work of God and be caught off guard by our enemy. We can be involved in such a zealous manner that it will hinder us from seeing what is not the will of God, but the deception of the devil. Perhaps the deception can be detected before it has caused any destruction to one's self or the life of others. Maybe it has lingered for months or even years. It may be ongoing now! Whichever the case, we are still able to redeem the time!

Obedience balanced with our love by our hope, coupled with our continuous focus and revisitation of the previous balances will deter, hinder, and in most cases prevent Satan's deception. We were born of man and that concludes us as sinners. The flesh was cursed and we dwell in the flesh. Therefore, we are well aware that there is nothing we can do to keep ourselves sinless for the rest of our lives. However, that should not prevent us from striving for a sinless life. We know that we are not going to ever be sinless as Jesus was. Nonetheless, He is our standard and we should strive for nothing less than what He represented. The octagon of spiritual balances is given to those of us who hate sin and want to do something about it and its deception in their lives so that they will receive a closer walk with God.

The octagon of spiritual balances ensures that we will ascertain and retain our spiritual makeup and our spiritual awareness as we stand in light of the enemy's agenda for the children of God, which is to steal, kill, and destroy. Furthermore, it will prevent sin in our lives and restrict us from exalting ourselves. Yet it will keep us focused on our God and Lord Jesus the Christ.

To define obedience; it is when one submits to a request or a command. For example, when Jesus told the people in John 6:27 to "labour not for the meat which perisheth, but for that meat which endureth unto everlasting life," they, in the twenty-eighth verse asked, "What shall we do, that we might work the works of God?" Jesus told them in the twenty-ninth verse, "This is the work of God, that ye believe on him whom he sent. The apostle John repeated God in 1 John 3:23 when he said, "And this is his commandment, that we should believe on the name of his son Jesus Christ."

If we are going to obey God, we must first "believe on him whom he sent" (John 6:29). Without this first step, we cannot obey His perfect will because God's will, first and foremost, is for us to believe in His son Jesus the Christ.

There are those who are deceived and believe they will be accepted by God and are able to do the will of God and bypass His Son in doing so. I say to you very emphatically and without reservation that that cannot be done.

Some believe they have the favor of God while they recognize His Son as merely a man, perhaps a prophet or even a little god. There are others who believe that the Christ has not come and are still awaiting his arrival. Yet they believe that they are actively serving God.

Those who believe in this manner do not understand the truth, especially that of redemption. How sad it is to witness this deception of Satan. Many hearts and minds are veiled in error because of the lack of knowledge.

Our obedience begins with believing in Jesus the Christ, His birth, death, and resurrection as well as His divinity, God the Word incarnate.

For us to believe in Jesus, we must also believe in the written word of God. In the Gospel of John 1:1, 14, we are told, "In the beginning was the word, the word was with God, and the word was God," "And the word was made flesh, and dwell among us." In 1 Timothy 3:16, God tells us, "And without controversy great is the mystery of godliness: God was manifest in the flesh."

If we cannot accept and believe this truth, everything else in the Bible is useless. We can set the Bible aside and do what is right in our eyes.

It is the word of God which we must accept and believe and that is to believe and accept Jesus as God, not just as our Lord and savior, but also as God. Titus 2:13–14 reads as follows, "Looking for that blessed hope, and the glorious appearing of the great God and our Saviour Jesus Christ; Who gave himself for us that he might redeem us." We must observe and note that the singular pronouns himself and he used in verse 14 is identifying one person. Therefore, the phrase denotes the great God and our savior Jesus Christ as being one person. This is the teachings of the word of God!

Without this acceptance, what we obey is of the same design as the instincts of any animal. Our love is imaginary, our hope is to no avail, and trust is in what we imagine. Faith and belief does not exist, and knowledge and spiritual understanding are psychological fabrications. Life does not have a balance and will always lack stability and harmony. But more importantly, there cannot be life after the death of the flesh!

Obedience of the word of God fortifies all balances. Without proper obedience to the word of God, definite indications of an imbalance is recognized by spiritual weakness, confusion, disharmony, instability, fear, or even pride, which will also prevent us from progressing spiritually. The same imbalance which causes spiritual disarray will be found in one of the previous balances or factors as we revisit them in search for what hinders us.

What can cause us to believe that Jesus is not God? I continue this subject matter because without believing Jesus is God, there is no such thing as truth to have any knowledge. There is nothing to give faith, trust, hope or even love. Therefore, obedience has no essential spiritual quality in life.

Our belief develops from what is known to us, what we are sure of, what we have confidence in, and what we have conviction of. We call this confidence, conviction, and faith. And faith comes from knowledge of. However, if what knowledge we have lacks truth, our knowledge is deficient and unbelief prevails. So if it is knowledge that is needed to believe and we do not believe, then it is due to the lack of knowledge and truth.

If Satan is able to blind us and get us to believe that Jesus is not God and death comes prior to our understanding, hell awaits us. If we do not believe that Jesus is God and we are physically able to fulfill all other commandments, hell still awaits. Should Satan instill this deception in us, destruction is imminent. Nothing else matters if we cannot believe that Jesus is God!

Now that we understand that obedience starts with accepting and believing that Jesus is God, we can proceed in perfecting our daily walk in God. In doing so, however, we must remain focused on the previous balances.

We would like to believe if our knowledge, faith, trust, hope and love are intact, it will become easy to obey God. Nonetheless, we must in all situations and circumstances revisit the balances. The enemy is always trying to tempt us, deceive us, and confuse us. The devil will use our feelings, emotions, desires, and basic needs to cause our understanding of a situation to move us, causing us to believe that we are in obedience of God.

He will twist, add, or delete from the scriptures as he did with Eve when he said to her in Genesis 3:4, "Ye shall not surely die." He misrepresented what God told Adam, and it altered what they originally believed. The consequence of that deception is the existence of death until the end of time.

The zeal to do the work of God coupled with erroneous input will mutate our faith, causing an imbalance in our belief and trust polluting our hope and love and; subsequently, it will initiate an action not originating from God. This is why we must disregard our feelings and emotions and ask, is this what I am hearing from God, am I being deceived, did it come from the outside or from within, does it cause a ripple, and is it contrary to the word of God?"

Remember what God said in 1 John 4:1, "Believe not every spirit, but try the spirits whether they are of God." So reevaluate what you know, especially the current situation or circumstance. Ask yourself, does my faith come from my knowledge, am I truly hearing directly from God, and is my belief balanced with my faith?

This is imperative because we respond to what we have faith and believe in. Our trust, hope, love, and obedience are based on what we hear from God, whereby our faith and belief are derived. Should our faith be moved by an entity other than God and we step into the obedience mode without checking, it could cause irreversible damage, even destruction to ourselves or to others.

Separate yourself and learn to detect the difference between Satan's deception and God's voice. God has told us to be sure of His unction and requires us to test the validity of our spiritual direction.

If uncertainty and confusion lingers, knowing that God is not the author of confusion, any action taken besides waiting on an indisputable answer from God is acting on the probability of chance. Because we have such difficulties discerning the voice of God, we must come to understand that God leads us by our daily faith more often than not.

God causes, allows, or disallows events, situations or circumstances in the life of the believer for His purpose. Our feelings, emotions, needs, desires, and even our zeal hinder us at times from hearing and understanding the voice of God. So He does what He knows best for us, and at times, it requires some inconveniences, trials, tribulations, and sufferings, which only He can understand.

There are so many believers who believe that they have heard the voice of God and attempt to obey that which they heard, resulting in an ill-affected or negative outcome. They in turn, justify their action instead of admitting that they have been deceived by the enemy. This allows the enemy to continue with additional courses of deception because the believer is prideful, indicating an expressed imbalance and does not want to admit to error. This inspires Satan's ambition as it gives him a greater foothold in the believer's life.

However, this does not prevent God from speaking to us and giving us a spiritually conscious awareness of His presence, power, and leadership. We know that He is God, He is able, and He can accomplish what pleases Him even through our weak flesh.

Hear what God said He will do to His people in Ezekiel 36:26–27. He said:

> A new heart also will I give you, and a new spirit will I put within you: and I will take away the stony heart out of your flesh, and I will give you

an heart of flesh. And I will put
my spirit within you, and cause
you to walk in my statues, and
ye shall keep my judgments,
and do them.

Remember where God reigns, certainty abounds
and confidence is manifested in the heart and mind
of the believer; whereas, the believer is moved in obedience by the Holy Spirit to accomplish what the
Lord desires. Therefore, the next factor of the octagon of spiritual balances is introduced to the believer.

CHAPTER 7

W hen our obedience is under the unction of the Holy Spirit, it will accomplish that which pleases God. If we have surrendered our lives to God and our love for Him is balanced, His will and His way will become our highest priority in life.

Upon the accomplishment of obedience, a peace will fall upon us that defies explanation and brings us to the next spiritual balance. This spiritual balance will use our love for God as the balancer of our obedience which ushers in peace. Our obedience, if of God, will induce peace, and both will be balanced by our love.

Peace, the peace that we are searching for is found in John 14:27, and it tells us of its origin and its characteristics. Jesus said, "Peace I leave with you, my peace I give unto you: not as the world giveth, give I unto you. Let not your heart be troubled, neither let it be afraid."

This peace that comes to us from Jesus is a peace of mind, a tranquility with a sense of divine favor. In addition, it is a peace that is supernaturally given and felt, a peace which causes us to sense the presence of God within our spirit, which will result in the same peace encompassing our entire being. This peace that is within us will cause us to think peace and walk peace regardless of our surroundings.

This peace is a peace of mind, which when not in conjunction with the spirit is controlled by the effects of our senses. However, when Jesus gives us peace, even what comes through our senses cannot affect our peace. Therefore, this peace has placed our spirit, soul, and body in one accord through the work of the Holy Spirit.

This peace goes beyond our confidence, conviction, and expectation. This peace, which is within, increases our spiritual understanding of God's divine protection. There is no fear, and the absence of confusion is beyond description. Sorrow cannot touch this peace, and evil cannot penetrate its spiritual ambience.

This peace is granted to us from Jesus through our obedience to His will. God tells us in Proverbs

3:1–2, "My son forget not my law; but let thine heart keep my commandments: For length of days, and long life, and peace, shall they add to thee."

Should we surrender our lives and give God's will first priority, we will receive peace that surpasses human understanding. However, if we perform the will of God reluctantly, which is displeasing to Him, peace will not be present. We will find ourselves as miserable as Jonah was after he disobeyed God when told to go to Nineveh and actually went in the opposite direction. Jonah did not surrender himself to the will and way of God, so his rebellion did not produce the peace which Jesus gives, a peace to this day that most believers are unaware of.

Obedience is an act and peace is a feeling of spiritual delight. There may be a time when God will tell us to step into action and obey. There may also come a time when God will tell us as He did in Psalm 46:10, to "be still and know that I am God." God is not telling us to do absolutely nothing, to be passive or to become complacent but rather stop working on our own and seek Him.

There are far too many Christians who believe that they need to physically be involved in a task while all God wants them to do is be still and come to know that He is God. In other words, get to know Him as God and familiarize yourself with His will and His way. Without knowing God and His will, we cannot obey. If we are working in the name of the Lord without knowledge, we are obviously doing what we think God would have us to do, and that is not His will. It is the will of the enemy!

Therefore, an imbalance exists even if we claim to have peace. That imbalance may cause the believer to have peace, but I assure you that it is a false peace. It is a deception of Satan, attempting to keep us in his will by instilling a false perception of peace.

This peace comes from the outside, this peace comes by the way of the world, and this peace is temporal. It is not protective. It does not possess a sense of assurance, and it is not absolute. This peace is not real for it will pass away as will time and this world shall pass away. That is why our peace must be in Jesus for He is from everlasting to everlasting, and He has overcome the world.

Those who continue to practice iniquity and claim peace are deceived. Seeking peace outside of obedience to the will of God is futile and delusive. As stated in chapter 6, God's preeminent will for us comes from the Gospel of John 6:29, "That ye believe on him whom he hath sent." God repeated this in the letter of 1 John 3:23, "And this is his commandment, That we should believe on the name of his son Jesus Christ." The peace that we seek from Jesus can only come from us believing Him, that is, committing ourselves to Him, trusting, obeying, hoping, and loving all of who He is and setting His desires above our fleshly desires.

If our trust, hope, and love for Him are not balanced, our lack of peace will be evident. When the lack of peace surfaces and if we are absolutely honest with ourselves, we will realize that there is an imbalance with one or more of the previous factors or balances.

The imbalance may be found in our obedience. Perhaps what may have been performed with an expectation of abounding peace may not have been the work or the will of God. And consequently, we may have been deceived. This will be a problem with most Christians because we do not care to believe that we can be deceived by the enemy. However, it happens to every Christian at some time or another.

If we continue to deny our weakness and vulnerability to deception, we actually enhance Satan's grip in our lives. When we admit to our weaknesses and other spiritual infirmities, it does not give us a license to continue, and it is not a statement condoning sin, but instead it gives us a conscious awareness of Satan's avenues of attack. Therefore, it is spiritually healthy to seek and admit errors, weaknesses, and imbalances.

It is only at that time, we can successfully fight the wiles of the enemy. Why? Because we are now able to admit, at least to ourselves, that we have some type of spiritual infirmity and in doing so through the strength of the Holy Spirit, we are now able to fight, defeat, and claim the victory.

Our imbalance may be found in our love for God or the lack thereof. It may be in our hope, which will explain why our love was not sufficient, and the balance of obedience and peace were not attained. It may be in our trusting Him, and again this will tell us why our hope and love were not balanced. The search for the imbalance will determine the discord as we revisit our spiritual balances. It will help us defeat the plans of the enemy, put him in check, balance what was out of balance, and strengthen our walk in God.

Peace is another check point in the believer's life. If true peace prevails, that peace from within which encompasses our entire being and increases our spiritual understanding of God's divine protection, then the peace which surpasses human understanding will be dominant. However, we must be honest with ourselves again as to whether what we have endeavored to perform is the true work and will of God.

If we have not reached this point, it is a definite indication of an imbalance, and we need to revisit and examine our balances and factors until we attain spiritual equilibrium. When we receive true peace, we will experience an overwhelming joy, which will place us in such a state of spiritual bliss and tranquility that our desire will be to forever remain its captive.

With that spiritual expectation in mind, we can now go to the eighth and final balance of the octagon of spiritual balances.

CHAPTER 8

Peace   *Joy*

Obedience

This final balance is the highest spiritual expectation a believer can receive here on Earth. This balance is comprised of peace and joy which will be balanced by our obedience.

We must first recognize that our obedience will be what we rely on to fulfill our peace and joy. That is why it is imperative that our obedience is the work and will of God, and it should be tested and be indisputable, prior to pursuing a task or attempting to perform what comes into our mind. Remember what God told us in 1 John 4:1, "Beloved, believe not every spirit, but try the spirits whether they are of God."

The fulfillment of balancing our peace and joy will in turn promote us to the highest level attainable on behalf of the believer. To know this is a consolation to the believer who may be just starting the Christian walk as well as the seasoned believer. Merely to know that there is a purpose, a mission, and a destination that is attainable will give the believer the determination to press forward with great expectation.

This joy, as stated at the end of chapter 7, is overwhelming. However, peace and joy, together and balanced, encompasses and overwhelms the believer with such spiritual exultation that the believer is placed in a state of spiritual metamorphosis, absorbing all of the spiritual benefits and rewards of obedience. That the believer emerges with a greater understanding and longing to continually obey the word of the Lord with a constant desire to return to that spiritual state and remain as long as eternity is eternal.

Now this will apply to each situation and circumstance. The believer may have peace and joy balanced in one area of life, but in another, there may still remain an imbalance. If the believer was able to attain harmony in one area, then it is possible to successfully attain it in another. There will always be an area in the believer's life that will need to be balanced. But the good news is, it can be done!

We, who believe, can attain and maintain more of an increased and balanced spiritual life if we only focus on the octagon of spiritual balances.

I would not have anyone ignorant regarding this book. It is not this writing that will give you the necessary spiritual balance. It is the effort that the believer puts forth to attain that which God wants to give us. It is the help, power, and sufficiency of the Holy Spirit who dwells within the believer that overcomes all obstacles and produces what pleases God.

The believer can use these principles as an avenue and a measuring stick for growth. It can also become a focal point toward our spiritual objectives and goal. However, we must remember we must always and foremost be honest with ourselves.

If we attempt to manifest joy in an area of our life when in actuality the balance is not there, we will only be fooling ourselves and giving Satan additional ground. We need to identify the imbalance, put Satan in check, balance what is out of balance and joy will usher itself in. Do not attempt to force a factor in place if it is subjectively out of balance. An imbalanced factor is an indication of insufficiency and the need for correction in the believer's life.

Joy as well as the previous factors can be balanced under all sorts of situations and circumstances. We need not think that all things must be convenient and favorable for the believer. Balances and their factors can be attained and maintained in the seasons of poverty, fiery trials, loss, imprisonment, tribulation, and persecution at home, on the job, and during recreation.

If we are looking at a situation or person to develop our joy, then our focus is not where it should be. Our concentrated effort should be on the work of Jesus and our absolute certainty that we are obeying His will. The result will be divine joy!

However, we must allow God to do what He does the best. It is God's responsibility to make the necessary changes in our lives, for only He can. We are only vessels, vehicles, tools, and instruments of God to deliver His word and define the example in our Christian walk. He does the changing!

He quickens the spirit, He initiates a desire to know Him, He instills confidence and convicts us of truth, and He grants us the ability to trust Him. He bestows hope and expectation as His love for us causes our love for Him to abound. His will and His way supplant ours, and ultimate peace and joy emerges.

Listen to what God said about His Son in Hebrews 12:2, "Looking unto Jesus the author and finisher of our faith; who for the joy that was set before him endured the cross." The joy that was set before Jesus sustained Him as He endured the cross for our sake.

Jesus tells us in John 15:1–11 that He is the vine, God is the husbandman, and we are the branches. He abides in the love of the Father by obeying His commandments, and we will abide in His love by keeping His commandments.

There are three reasons why Jesus told us to abide in Him first, He said, "For without me you can do nothing," second, "that my joy might remain in you," and third, "that your joy might be full." Yes, Jesus has a great concern regarding our joy. He understands our need for joy, for it was His expectation of ultimate joy that strengthened Him to endure the cross.

He told us in John 17:13, "Now I come to thee and these things I speak in the world, that they might have my joy fulfilled in themselves." Jesus wants us to have this joy, His joy, in its fullness. It is the same joy that sustained Him.

This joy is available to those believers who the Holy Spirit dwells within and of those who put forth the effort to seek the knowledge required of God the Father, God the Son, and God the Holy Spirit. Obedience to the word of God will confirm the impartation and balance of spiritual understanding, knowledge, faith, belief, trust, hope, love, peace, and joy.

Without balancing all of the factors of the octagon of spiritual balances, it is not possible to reach that point where peace and joy will continually increase in the life of the believer. Without a complete balance, we will never comprehend what Jesus has promised, even knowing that it is attainable!

There were many times when I asked God, how can a man die to himself and live simultaneously for Jesus? How can a man get from the point of spiritual death to spiritual exultation? I continued to pray and I continued to ask probably for years. But when I asked the Lord for help, He appointed a time for spiritual exultation to encompass me.

It came during an inconvenient, unfavorable, and uncomfortable time in my life. However, when He incorporated His joy in my life, it surpassed everything else, and I have had numerous experiences of the same type of spiritual exultation since.

Every time we balance these spiritual factors in each situation and circumstance, we will receive spiritual exultation as if it was a reward for surrendering to the will and way of God. But we must also remember that it is not of us or it is not about us. It is of God and about God through the indwelling work of the Holy Spirit.

When the octagon of spiritual balances are in effect in our daily lives; a complete spiritual balance is established. A spiritual success has been attained, and total spiritual victory can be proclaimed by the believer.

When God revealed this pattern of events that led to spiritual exultation on my behalf, He allowed me to experience the progression of expectation and subsequent spiritual exultation many times as if He was proving to me its efficacy. He then enabled me as His instrument to share with you His instructions toward achieving spiritual completeness by way of "The Octagon of Spiritual Balances."

My prayer is that you will receive what the Lord has made known unto you and allow the Holy Spirit to lead you as He led me through the orchestration and completion of this spiritually effectual edification.

About the Author

Pastor Bernard J. Weathers is the pastor of Word of Faith Ministries, in Colonia, New Jersey. For ten years, he studied the word of God in a small room converted into a study, where he became well acquainted with the true and living God.

He was disciplined under the direction of the Holy Spirit and a tremendous change came over him as it was evident to all who knew him God was at work. Miracles began to occur in his life and the life of immediate family members as his faith steadily increased.

He enrolled in an extended Bible college and obtained a bachelor degree in religious education and a master degree in theology. During the years he attended classes, he labored to perfect a profound teaching ministry employing his gift of teaching, which is empowered by the Holy Spirit. He has taught a comprehensive and intensely instructive Bible study for the past eighteen years.

Pastor Weathers is an anointed teacher of the Word, a loving, disciplined, and godly man who has a profound love for his congregation and all those called under the ministry of the Lord Jesus. Pastor Weathers possesses exceptional leadership qualities, but above all, he is a man who surrendered to God's sovereign authority and has committed with an unwavering devotion to the work of Christ, the furtherance of the gospel, and the understanding of divine revelation.

CPSIA information can be obtained
at www.ICGtesting.com
Printed in the USA
BVOW03s1202171116
468182BV00001B/1/P